THE ROAD TO CONTROLLING YOUR CAREER

The question is not are there jobs available?
The question is, are you prepared to get the available jobs?

Ty C. Ferrell Sr.

Order this book online at www.trafford.com
or email orders@trafford.com

Most Trafford titles are also available at major online book retailers.

Printed in the United States of America.

ISBN: 978-1-4269-7553-0 (sc)
ISBN: 978-1-4269-7554-7 (e)

Library of Congress Control Number: 2011912574

Trafford rev. 09/14/2011

 www.trafford.com

North America & international
toll-free: 1 888 232 4444 (USA & Canada)
phone: 250 383 6864 ♦ fax: 812 355 4082

CONTENTS

INTRODUCTION

Congratulations! By reading this guide, you have taken the second step toward getting your dream job.

You may be thinking, what was the first step? That was making the decision to do the research and gather all the information you could to help land the position you have been seeking.

While it is true that the procedures in this book will be a great benefit to job seekers of all ages, the primary purpose of this book is to help baby boomers land their dream job. The Road to Controlling Your Career will help baby boomers to achieve two critical goals. 1- Identify and organize your skills and achievements. 2- Be able to articulate those skills and achievements in an interview and as part of your elevator speech (commercial).

For those who are employed while looking for another job, you must make the time to complete the proven processes and procedures we will cover in this guide. Remember, we are not talking about going for any job available; we are talking about you getting your dream job.

We will cover how to build a winning resume, how to create a Cover letter, constructing your "Elevator Speech" (" your commercial") and developing a Thank you letter. You will also learn a great process for preparing for the interviews.

We will cover different types of interviews you may go through during your job search. We will review some important points on body language. Included is an extensive list of common interview questions. There is also a great section on how to impress the interviewer with answers that put you in the best possible light and will keep the focus on your skills.

Finally, we will cover how to negotiate your starting salary.

Now, let's get started on the steps that will lead you to your dream job.

CHAPTER 1

Building Your Resume

There are important documents you need to build before you go to any interview. I use the term "build" because this procedure requires a lot of research, critical thinking and condensing all of your experiences and skills into a few pages. It starts with building an impressive resume that grabs the attention of potential employers.

It is my intention to offer enough help through this guide for anyone to build a strong resume and give a command performance in any interview. It is imperative that you have a well-constructed resume ready before you start interviewing.

Here are the generic or basic components you will need for any interview.

Resume

Core Competencies

Objective Statement

Cover letter / Application letter

Elevator speech/commercial

Thank you letter

I am a firm believer that all your focus should be on completing one segment at a time. You will find each completed segment will help you construct the next part of your interview package.

The Resume

A resume is a brief recap of who you are and what you have accomplished in your life. Another term for resume is Curriculum Vitar (CV) or Vita, so if you see those terms in any document just know it means resume.

The resume is a critical part of your overall interview package that will help you respond properly to questions you will get from an interviewer.

Thorough knowledge of your resume will help you stay focused on your best attributes and skills as well as help the interviewer see how you will fit in the position. Were you ever asked in an interview to talk about yourself or how you handled an issue? How long did it take you to answer? Interviewers may perceive hesitation negatively, as if you are making it up on the spot. Did you have a good example of a situation that you handled well? Remembering things you have not thought about for some time can be tough. After the interview, when you thought about your answers, did you ask yourself 'what on earth was I thinking'?

You will avoid these problems by spending as much time as needed focusing on your competencies and practicing how to articulate them in an interview. A well-constructed resume is a great study guide to practice interviewing.

You should look at your resume as the first and maybe the most important interview. Your resume is tantamount to an interview, the most critical document you will construct as part of your job seeking, eventually you'll have to ask yourself, " what skill sets do I have'. What would make me an invaluable part of this team? Your resume can get you into an interview or keep you out.

When a company receives your resume, it will be one of many. Will your resume stand out and be memorable? This guide is to make sure the answer is YES!

Your resume must be a well-constructed document of your qualifications, experience and academic achievements that will compel the reader to want to know more about you; like a well written book that keeps a reader turning the pages. Your resume must also be relevant to the position you are seeking. Example, if your background is an office manager and you are seeking a department manager position in a retail store, speak to your leadership and organizational skills overall and not specifically about the industry from whence you came. The purpose of this guide is to point out just how important your resume is in job seeking. Far too many people see the resume as just something they need to put together to go along with whatever else they may need for an interview. I cannot say this strongly enough; without an outstanding resume, there most likely will not be an interview. You must view job seeking as a full time job itself. The more time and attention you put into it, the better your outcome. Remember, we are talking about you controlling your destiny.

There is so much to say about how to create a winning resume, rather than re-write the book I will suggest a good path to begin. Here are the basic parts of a resume

- **Contact / Identifying Information**
- **Career Objective Statement**
- **Experience / Employment History / Skills**
- **Awards / Honors**
- **Education**

Blank page for your notes

The Body of the Resume

Experience / Employment History / Skills

In this section of the resume, you will tell the potential employer what companies you have worked with and the positions you have held. You will also give a brief history of your responsibilities and accomplishments that correspond with each job. The key here is brevity. Brevity is very important because a wordy document could lose the reader, be an irritant and/or lead the reader to think you will not get right to the job.

Hiring managers may scan over your resume for buzzwords or phrases that quickly clarify you as a possible good fit for the position. A wordy document gives greater opportunity to say something you should not. Finally, this section of your resume is to show what you did, where you did it and when you do it. Not how you did it. A more detailed explanation on your work history is what takes place in the interview not on the resume.

Buzzwords are important because when you submit your resume on line, some organizations use a computer application that scans for such buzzwords that match their need as the resume is downloaded and absent that kind of connection, your resume may not go any farther.

Some examples of buzzwords and phrases you should consider using are, implemented, developed, coached, led team, coordinated, organized and managed.

'How to layout your employment section'

Arrange this section of your resume in reverse chronological order beginning with your current or most recent position.

There are several possible layouts for this section and any one of them would do just fine. It is very important to be consistent, if you have several jobs to list, each one should follow the same format. Here is an example of a basic layout that works well:

COMPANY NAME

(Big World Sales Corp.)

Your Position   Dates you worked (from – to)

(General Manager)   (June 2007 to May 2010)

List your duties, responsibilities, results and accomplishments here.

When speaking about your results and accomplishments, include numbers and percentages if necessary.

Example;
- 'Oversee hiring, training and development of 235 associates'
- 'Implemented sales contest that led to $350.000 increase for the quarter'.
- 'Reduced overall expenses 6.0% for the year by coaching team on improving controllable expenses '.

Using brief concise sentences include all positive results for each position you list. Give the most information for your most recent job and any of the positions most relevant to the position you are seeking. One important point to remember when creating this section is you should consider all possible skills you may have used. For example, if you were a part of a team although not the leader but were instrumental in reaching a goal, you should include it as an accomplishment (Teamwork).

If you have held several jobs, you need only focus on the last ten years depending on how long you have been in the workforce. However, be prepared to talk about older jobs if asked.

If you have very limited job experience or just completing school, focus on the education section making sure to include any additional training classes you have taken. In this case, you should also put more emphasis on what type of position you are looking for in your Objective Statement.

Core Competencies

The first component needed to start constructing your resume, your core competencies.

Core competencies are your areas of expertise, abilities, fundamental knowledge or skill sets that you have and make you a qualified candidate for a particular position. We all have these competencies but may not readily know how to articulate them when asked. That is because most people do not spend much time thinking about them; we just do what we do. This is a very important segment of your interview package. It will be the cornerstone to building the rest of your resume. Your objective statement, experience, skill set and qualification sections are all moving parts of your competencies.

Here is a great way to get to know your competencies, prioritize them and be able to communicate them verbally or in written form with just a moment's notice.

Here is what you need.

- **Pencil**
- **Notepad**
- **One hour of uninterrupted time to stay focused**
- **On a different day, use another hour of uninterrupted time to scrub (edit) your list**

Here is what to do.

Think about processes (skills) you have used with respect to getting things done and reaching goals. An important point to remember, you may use your true competencies (skills) in several places. For example, on the job you may make sure all tasks are completed on time. At home, a parent may make sure all homework assignments are completed and handed in on time. In the community, you may be on a committee and are instrumental in making sure your meetings start and stop at the proper times. All of those actions fall under a competency called time management.

Set aside the first hour and complete your lists of what you feel are your competencies.

(Blank sheet provided)

Think about the things you do well and list them all. The list should have twenty five to thirty competencies. On a different day set aside another hour to review your list several more times and start crossing out things that you do not think are real marketable competencies. You should end up with nine or ten very strong competencies (skills).

(Blank sheet provided)

Some basic competencies that employers look for are

> **Time management**
>
> **Leadership**
>
> **Organization**
>
> **Problem solving**
>
> **Follow up**

On a separate sheet of paper, make five columns using each of the competency headings just named.

(Blank sheets provided)

Write each one of your nine or ten competencies under the appropriate column. Going forward, these are the terms you should use when talking about you skills (competencies) with potential employers. This is the foundation that you will construct your resume from and will get you ready for **COMMAND PERFORMANCE INTERVIEWS**.

Blank Competency Sheet #1

Use this sheet to list your twenty-five to thirty competencies.

Blank Competency Sheet #2

Use this sheet to list your narrowed down list of nine or ten very strong competencies

Competency Catalog Sheet

Time management   Leadership   organization   Problem solving   Follow up

Objective Statement

After putting your competencies list together highlighting those that best fit the job you seek, the next step is creating an "Objective Statement." This statement consists of putting that information into a well-constructed attention-grabbing paragraph assuring any potential employer's further interest in you.

Adding an objective statement will tell the potential employer you have a clear understanding of what position you want as well as what skills you will bring to the company. A short paragraph of three or four sentences with meaningful descriptive words that project your image strongly will be very effective.

Your objective statement will be the bases for your response to many of the interviewer's questions. It is important to personalize your objective and tailor it to the position you are seeking.

Here is an example of what a completed competencies list might look like and will be the building blocks for your objective statement.

Leadership	**Time management**
Organization	**Problem solving**
Follow up	**motivating**
Teamwork	**Training**
Listening	**Analytical**

Blank page for your notes

Example of an Objective Statement

This applicant is applying for a management position with a retail company and has several years of experience in this particular position. After deciding which of these competencies, best fit the position the applicant is applying for the following is an example of how the objective statement may look.

The Completed Objective Statement

'Dynamic Operations Manager, focused on motivating and coaching others, looking to use my vast retail experience for a progressive company with a strong interpersonal and team building philosophy.

Here is the way the objective breaks down:

Dynamic Operations Manager (**That is who you are**)

Focused on motivating and coaching others (**This illustrates what you do and your leadership skills**)

Looking to use my vast retail experience (**This is what you bring to the position**) for a progressive company with a strong interpersonal and team building philosophy. (**This is the type of organization you are interested in working for**) this statement also tells the interviewer you know the organization believes in team building.

Again, this is why you need to spend as much time as possible putting your competencies list together. Your objective statement comes directly from that list. Your task is to turn that list into a brief highly descriptive autobiography about you.

The reader of your objective statement should understand the position you are interested in, the skills you have and how you may apply them to help the organization.

It is a good idea to have several objective statements on file and ready to insert into your resume. However, do not invent skills for any jobs. Honesty is the best policy. You should tailor your word choices, skills, and experiences to highlight how you fit the title and job description of each position you are seeking. Here is an example of using the same objective statement from above for a different position.

Objective Statement: (with small change)

Dynamic <u>Sales Team Manager</u> focused on motivating and coaching others. Looking to use my vast <u>leadership</u> experience for a progressive company with a strong interpersonal and team building philosophy.

These subtle changes will help the potential employer to visualize you in the position they are looking to fill.

After a potential employer reviews your resume, most of the questions they will ask you will relate to something they read in the resume. For example, they may say, "Tell me how you motivate and coach your team". In this case, they are asking you to talk about some of the competencies mentioned in the objective statement, where it said, "Focused on motivating and coaching others". Your answer will be right at hand because of the work and thought you put into building your competencies list.

It is very important that you practice communicating those skills effortlessly when answering any questions about yourself. They will be the major talking points of any interview.

Take your time constructing you objective statement. Once you have it completed, ask family or friends to review it and give their opinions. Be open to constructive criticism as their perspective could mirror potential employers.

Ty C. Ferrell Sr.

Blank page for your notes

Identification Information and Education Sections of the Resume

These are the easiest two sections of the resume to layout but are just as important as any other section.

First, we will look at the Identification Section.

This section holds all of your contact information in a very concise well-organized manner for potential employers. This section should include your full legal name (in bold), permanent address, home phone number, cell phone number and e-mail address. Place this section on the top of the page, normally centered or indented left.

Here is an example of a classic layout:

Your Name
Street Address
City, State and Zip Code
Home Phone, Cell Phone
E-mail Address

The Education Section

Your education section should be straightforward and concise. Include all schools, universities, and/or extra classes or courses you have completed. Be sure to include all degrees and any certificates along with completion dates. A GPA should only be included if you earned a 3.0 or higher. Do not include high school information.

Education Section Example
- **Santana University**
- **Bachelor of Arts (business)   1989**

Add additional schools and degrees

(Optional) You can also list your computer skills under this section

Example
- **Computer Skills**
- **Word, access, publisher, power point and excel**

You can add other optional parts to your resume; this is not a recommendation, just informational. Keep in mind brevity is very important with a resume; however, if you have strong skills or credentials that fall under an optional section and they are relevant to the position, you may want to consider adding that particular section.

Here are some of the most common optional sections

- Summary of Achievements
- Summary of Qualifications and Skills – (must link back to the information in the body of your resume)
- Activities professional and non-professional
- Honors and Awards professional and school
- Community / Volunteer Work
- Leadership Activities
- Language Skills – (you can also just add this in the education section)

If you use optional sections, just use bullet points to name the skills, awards or credentials with a very brief statement of support if needed.

Example

Summary of Achievements

- Developed safety program that reduced injuries 12%
- Implemented training program on improving customer service that led to an 8% improvement in customer service rating
- Wrote a training seminar on a sales technique that increased sales by $850.000
- Designed cross training program for all department managers that increased overall productivity for the year

Black page for your notes

CHAPTER 2

Cover Letter

Is having a cover letter important? Yes!

It is a good idea to keep an updated cover letter on file at all times, here is why. Whether you are in the camp with those that say cover letters are old school and no longer needed or you believe you should send a cover letter with every resume, here is a simply fact of life; when you apply to a position on line, many corporations require you to summit your cover letter along with your resume. So if you do not believe in cover letters, good luck explaining that to them.

Your cover letter will most likely be the first communication the potential employer will read about you. The purpose of the cover letter is to tell the employer why you are sending your resume to them and leave him or her eager to review your resume.

Writing a cover letter may seem daunting to many job seekers. Look at it this way, your cover letter is a brief concise explanation of your resume (your history). The cover letter tells the potential employer what skills, experiences and abilities you have that match the qualifications they are seeking. Your cover letter should also explain why you are interested in working for this particular organization.

Your cover letter should be specific to each position you are applying too. You can do this by reviewing the qualifications the corporation has listed for the position and highlight your skills that meet those qualifications in your cover letter.

Much like your objective statement and resume were constructed from your core competencies, your cover letter should be a brief culmination of those three documents.

Example of a Cover letter

Your Name
Your Street Address
City, State, Zip Code
Telephone Numbers
E-Mail Address
Date

Dear Mr. /Ms. / (You should have a name to address) To Whom It May Concern is never a good idea.

First paragraph should tell why you are writing; some basic information about you and how you heard about the position.

The second paragraph should demonstrate that you have done your research on the corporation, understand what the qualifications for the position are and why you feel you're a good candidate for the position by adding more details about the skills and experiences that the resume covers and how your background is very relevant to their needs. Make it clear that you are very interested in working with this organization. Do not duplicate your resume here but do mention your enclosed resume will further detail the corporations you have worked with along with the dates. Keep in mind you must include the buzz words for the position in case the corporation uses a scanner before human eyes get their chance to review the document.

The third and final paragraph should convey how much you are looking forward to an opportunity to interview with the corporation and further discuss the possibility of joining their team. It is a good idea to let them know you will follow up with them along with a time line for your follow up. Close the paragraph by thanking them for his or her time and consideration.

Close the letter with,

Sincerely or Regards
Your Name

(If your contact information is not at the top of the letter, it should go under your name)

Blank page for your notes

CHAPTER 3

Elevator Speech/Commercial

An elevator speech (also referred to as your commercial) simply means being able to give a brief oral presentation or description of you and what you do. This speech is about two minutes on average, (About the time it takes to go from the bottom floor to the top floor in an elevator in the average office building) and must touch on your work history, skills, accomplishments and your objective. Your speech must be intense enough to pull the person you are speaking with into the moment where he or she is able to quickly process and appreciate what you are saying. When your speech is over, you want them eager to hear more about you. Here are some challenges to this process.

How do you convey in some cases, years of accomplishments in mere seconds?

Answer: Pull all the information about yourself and your accomplishments together, and put all of the talking points into an outline. Use that outline as a study guide. Go over it several times and chip away at un-needed information, points and words that do not add value or impact to you telling a short memorable story about yourself. Cutting non- essential verbiage, practicing and timing yourself are the keys to success for this process. Another good way of staying focused on what information you need to give as well as how much time you have, is to think about calling a major corporation wanting to speak with a very busy Vice President that you may not have an appointment with. The receptionist that answers the phone is going to ask two question before he or she makes a decision about putting your call through or not. A- Who is calling? B- What is the nature of your call? The thought process you would use to make sure the receptionist puts your call though to the Vice President is the same thought process you need to develop a great elevator speech.

How do you do this without sounding as if you are bragging and tooting your own horn?

Answer: Throw those thoughts out of you mind. If you do not brag and toot your own horn in an interview, who will? If you do not believe you are the best candidate for the position, why should the interviewer?

What information should go into your speech and where will you get it?

If you follow all the steps out lined in this guide, you have all the documents and information you need to develop your elevator speech. That is, **your Resume, Core Competencies, Objective Statement and your Cover letter.**

Finally, look at your "elevator speech" as you would a movie trailer or preview, it must be a strong impactful story that compels the viewer or listener to want to see or hear the entire package. To do that, your speech must be very interesting and clearly shows your qualifications are a great match to the positions requirements. Remember, your speech is not solely about you, it is about what you can do for the corporation.

Blank page for your notes

CHAPTER 4

Different Types Of Interviews

The first and most difficult assignment you will have for any great job is the interview itself. If you do not give a great interview, you will not get that great job.

You should prepare for your interview with the same focus, organization and planning as you would for any important task or assignment you will have on any job. Did you know there are over a dozen different types of interviews? You should have a basic understanding of the most common types. With the ability to identify which type the interviewer is using, you will do a much better job of handling the task. This may sound rather daunting but this section will help you be better prepared and gain more confidence to give a command performance. Here you will find a brief helpful narrative on different types of interviews.

Traditional Interview

This style is the most common of all interviews, hence, the name Traditional Interview. You will most likely speak with one interviewer; however, a second party could sit in as well. If a second party does sit in during the interview, keep in mind he or she is there for a reason. This person could be present for training purposes and/or to give a second opinion. It is very important to establish a rapport with the interviewer because this individual may be the one that makes the hiring decision or refer you to the person who will. Do not take this type of interview lightly. Depending on the organization, this interview could be the only one given before the hiring decision. You must show enthusiasm, your qualifications as well as your willingness and ability to perform the job. Be sure your responses include your strong points, skills and abilities. Practicing how to articulate your skills as part of answering interview questions is a good idea.

Behavioral / Assessment Interview

This can be a standalone interview, integrated into any other types of interviews or in most cases as part of an online application. In a face-to-face interview using this process, you may not be aware it is an assessment. If this is the case, you can generally identify an assessment by the way the interviewer asks the questions. This is a fact-based procedure and the interviewer will start most questions with

"How did you handle...?"
"Tell me about a time when..." or
"Give me an example of..."

In this case, the interviewer wants to hear about real issues you have faced as well as how you resolved them. Your answers to these questions will indicate how you may react in the future. When answering behavioral questions, the interviewer is looking for the type of answers found in the organization's operational handbook and will be listening intently for details. This does not mean you need to know everything in the handbook, but consider how the company you are interviewing for would want you to handle those issues. Your answers must be concise and complete, supplying who, what, when and how as well as the resolution; or the interviewer may probe for more details.

On Line Assessment

Usually, you will know it is an assessment before you begin the process when it is on line.

An online assessment will seem easy because you will be answering yes or no and true or false questions. On the other hand, there is usually a time limit to the assessment. If you start moving too fast, you could misunderstand a question's true meaning and give a poor answer. Assessments give the company some insight into such key factors as your personality, honesty, customer service skills and problem solving as well as leadership skill and stress management. You may see the same question asked several different ways. It is very important to read each question carefully before answering.

Structured Interview

In its purest form, this type of interview is basic and straightforward. The interviewer will be asking you questions from a standardized list of questions most likely put together and collaborated on by human resource and several department heads. The key purpose of this interview is to zero in on whether you have the job skills and competencies essential for the position. It can be a long process with several parts. Here are some examples of the skills tested for: verbal, written, decision-making, time management, honesty, team building and interpersonal. The interviewer is looking for how you handle observation, personnel, situations and leadership. Most companies will score each question on a 1 to 10 scale for the best comparison to other candidates. This interview is very formal with little chance of establishing any rapport with the interviewer. The most important factor here will be your answers. As with all interviews, it is important to do some research on the corporation before the interview so you can customize your answers more to the company's culture. This is not to say make up answers, this will help you use more of the terms the company uses when giving your answers.

Phone / Screening Interviews

Recruiters, human resource representatives or someone that is a part of the interview process but unable to meet with you face to face uses phone interviews. This is the easiest type of interview to go through. You can have all of the information you gathered to help you with the interview, on hand to reference and help keep you on point. In all other interviews, your answers must come from memory because you will be face to face with the interviewer. One critical element to stay focused on is your voice and the energy that you project. The interviewer cannot see you so you must be sure to convey your enthusiasm. This interview is used to screen out job seekers that are not a good fit for the position or, move those that seem qualified to the next step in the interview process. It is much like a Structured Interview because the interviewer will work from a list of prepared questions. This interview is to verify your resume, your skills, qualifications and personality traits. For this interview, you do not have to be the best candidate; the interviewer's objective is to find qualified applicants. However, if you feel there is key information about you, not covered during the interview, you can bring it up at the end of the interview when asked, "Do you have any questions?" Just remember, it is better to cover those points as you answer other questions during the interview.

Screening interviews are commonly the first in a battery of interviews you may go through for a position. Recruiters or agencies that view your resume may call to see if you are interested in a position they are working to fill. If you have interest, the recruiter will most likely set a later time to call back and conduct a phone/screening interview. It is not a good idea to allow a recruiter to go ahead and conduct a screening interview in a first cold call contact. You need to prepare for this interview much as you would for any other type of interview. A recruiter will commonly do this interview by phone. Typically, a time is set for you to do a phone interview before hand. This allows you time to prepare.

Case Study Interview

This is a probing interview designed to get right to the heart of your operating style and is used for management positions. You will receive a real life case study of a problem you have to resolve. In your resolution, the interviewer will be looking to see if you use certain skill sets, such as; listening, quick thinking, analysis, creativity and calmness under stress. The interviewer is not looking for you to come up with the best possible answer, but rather your leadership and problem solving abilities to work through the problems. The best answer will show your ability to understand the problem, identify the root cause, resolve the issue and insure the problem will not reoccur. Your answer should be a brief explanation of how you would work through the case. If the above skills are not evident in your answer, you will do poorly in this interview.

Group Interview

Companies that regularly hire several associates at the same time may use group interviews. This is a very generic process where a company representative speaks to everyone at the same time. In a compact format, they may outline some policies, company history, job description, company expectations and examples of scheduling. You may also fill out some paperwork and at some point; you will speak to a representative on a one-one basis to discuss any details of a more personal nature. Group interviews are for non-management positions.

Panel Or Committee Interview

I often describe this interview as performing on stage. You will be answering questions from several different department heads within the organization who relate to the position you are seeking. Panel interviews are used for candidates seeking management, leadership or stressful positions and will be one part, usually the last step in the overall interview process. The following are two examples of this process:

1) You may be in a room where each panel member will come to you. A variation on this will have you move to meet each panel member in different rooms. Most likely only one panel member will be in the room at a time and will speak with you until that person completes a list of questions. Then the next panel member will come to you or you will go to him or her and repeat the process until all panel members have met with you. There is normally a time limit for each panel member as well. It is likely that one of the interviewers (usually the H.R. representative) will give you reports or a case study and allow time for you to review. Then the interviewer will ask you what were the problems, what were the causes of the problems and how would you resolve them?

2) All panel members may be in the room with you at the same time. In this case, questions may come from any one of the panel members randomly. However, normally it is not meant to be a stress test so most likely, you will receive questions from one panel member at a time until he or she completes their list of questions before the next member starts speaking with you. If all panel members are in the room, as you address each person's questions, keep as much eye- to- eye contact as possible but it is important to make eye contact with other members from time to time while answering questions, even when you are not speaking with them. This may help them remember a perceived connection with you after the interview.

As with any interview, the key to success is doing your research and being well prepared to answer any questions no matter which procedure the panel chooses to use.

Lunch Or Dinner Interview

Most job seekers will not go through an interview of this type. In the event you receive an invitation to this type of interview, you are most likely close to an offer of employment! This type of interview may be used for management or leadership positions. Candidates invited to a lunch or dinner interview should not make the mistake of thinking it is going to be more casual than an interview that would have taken place in an office. You will need to prepare for this interview as diligently as you would for any other type of interview. In fact, even more so because you not only have to handle all of the complexities of a normal interview, you have the added responsibility of understanding and delivering proper meal etiquette. Traditionally, the interviewer that invites you to this type of interview wants to evaluate your social and interpersonal skills along with all the other factors analyzed in any interview.

After you have completed all of the normal preparation for the interview, I recommend reviewing table manners. If you know the location the interview will be taking place, go there before hand and get to know the environment including the menu and service style of the establishment. Stay away from ordering anything that will be messy to eat and only order water or soft drinks. (Exception, if it is a diner interview and several others are present, if everyone at the table is having a glass of wine, it is fine to join them in that scenario).

Video Interview

This type of interview can feel a lot like a phone interview but you would do well to remember you are on camera and visible to one or more people at all times. This process is most like a group interview where you will be answering questions from several interviewers. Although several people will interview you, commonly you will only see one at a time. After an interviewer has completed his or her questions, they will typically introduce the person you will be speaking with next and leave your view (remember, even when you do not see anyone on camera, someone may still see you). The next interviewer will appear on camera, reintroduce his or herself and begin asking questions. This process will continue until all parties involved have spoken with you.

Because you are on camera at all times, it is a good idea to interlock your fingers in front of you on the table. This will help you control your body language and unconscious fidgeting. Keep eye contact with the person on the screen as if you were in the same room.

Directive Interview

Also known as a Patterned Interview it is closely related to The Structured Interview. The interviewer will take you in a clear direction hence the name, Directive interview and is considered a good method for the corporation to compare candidates. The interviewer may come across as very rigid and unmoving in his or her manner. Do not let that throw you; this is their way of keeping the interview moving in the planned direction. The interviewer will be asking a series of set questions that are the same to each candidate to make comparisons easier. This may differ from the type of outlined questions in a structured interview, which is a list of questions created by the human resource and legal departments of the company. In this type of interview, the interviewer may develop his or her own set of questions. They may be a follow-up to a previous interview for clarification or more fact-finding. Depending on the interviewer's style, this can feel more like an interrogation than an interview. Again, do not let that throw you. You can still take back some control of the interview by the way you answer the questions. You can interject important points and skills that you feel the interviewer should know by skillfully making them a part of the answers you are giving to his or her set questions. If you are in this type of interview, do not try to befriend the interviewer. If they sense you are doing that, they may very well push you off by rapidly firing their questions at you. This type of interview is strictly to get at the facts and clarify some points, not to establish rapport. However, it would be a good idea to take note of the interviewer's demeanor because if you get the position, he or she may be someone you will be working with in some capacity.

Stress Interview

Stress Interviews are typically used for candidates seeking positions in stressful environments where deadlines are very commonplace such as, Wall Street, or positions working in customer service. Interviewers using this technique are trying to see how you would handle pressure and stressful situations. Signs of you being stress tested could be the interviewer seeming to be argumentative or sarcastic and very aggressive or you may be kept waiting before the interview starts. During the interview, the interviewer may lapse into a long silence trying to unnerve you. You can break the silence by asking (with a smile) do you need me to clarify my last answer. He or she may allow interruptions such as phone calls or people coming in and out of the room to speak with the interviewer and may even seem to be attacking you. The interviewer also may try to confuse you or may make mistakes and blame you. He or she may try many tactics to intimidate you. If you sense a stress test is accruing, focus on your body language and keep any movement to a minimum, keep good eye contact and hold a pleasant smile. The best defense for this type interview is being well prepared for the interview in general. If you have done your research and practiced answering interview question, you will do fine. Just think of it as being on stage and give a great performance.

Meandering / None Directive

As the name implies, this type of interview can and will move in any direction at any moment and can end up talking about almost anything , job related or not. The interviewer will ask very broad open -ended questions such as, tell me about yourself and let you talk as much as you want. This is a double-edged sword. The interviewer may not push you in any direction so there is a chance you may not bring up an important point about your qualifications or, your free-range conversation could reveal something that you did not intend. A good way to handle this type of interview is to make sure you have prepared your answers to possible questions as you would do for any interview but it is even more important here to help keep you on track. The interviewer is allowing you to have some control over the flow of this proceeding. Therefore, you may choose to bring up subject that you are comfortable with and want to talk about. Each of the answers or skills you wish to talk about should be in the form of a very short story. If each point includes who, what, why and how along with the resolution, the interviewer may be inclined to leave you in the driver's seat. Pitfalls to be mindful of are, if your stories sound too good to be true or are very vague with little detail, the interviewer may began to probe and become more directive. In any event, if you notice a change in the interviewer's approach, go with the flow and do not try to take back the lead. In this type of interview, it is very important that you ask questions and show a lot of interest in the position. The interviewer may base their final decision on how much enthusiasm you show. This type of interview is more likely to be used when a company is interviewing for non- management positions. However, as with most types of interviews, any interviewer can use the meandering interview at any time. For example, the interviewer may switch to meandering in the middle of a Structured Interview for reasons of his or her own. With this type interview, it is also important to establish good rapport with the interviewer. As with all interviews, proper preparation is the key to success.

The Working Interview

I know this may sound a little strange to some of you, but a Working Interview is indeed a type of interview, albeit, rare. While there is not a particular career or profession this type of interview is more likely to be given, it could be used for positions such as child care, teachers, personal trainers and industrial sales. This type of interview is comparable to how athletes and/or entertainers interview for positions, by literally trying-out for the position and show casing they have the skills for the job. While you may be engaged in this interview process for several hours, typically, you will not be paid for your time. Of course, the payoff is landing the job. Although a legitimate form of interview, I caution jobseekers to beware of scams. Scruple-less people may run an advertisement for a position and use a working interview to have a jobseeker complete a task while knowingly benefiting having the jobseeker's preform a task with no intention of providing a job offer. You may be thinking 'isn't that illegal?' However, how many people would pursue the issue or even recognize the scam? "Buyer beware."

How to Avoid Scams

The answer is simple. If you follow all of the procedures in the chapter 'Preparing for The Interview,' you will know enough about the organization to make an intelligent decision about moving forward with this company or not.

How to Handle Yourself in a Working Interview

In this type of interview, the interviewer wants to see you in the role and working as you would if you already had the position. If you are applying for a position that is similar to your current or past position, simply do exactly what you are or have done previously. Just be yourself. If this position is new and something you will be doing for the first time, you can still hit a home run by doing your homework. Research what the position is including how it is performed and, if possible, visit with someone working in the position for direct experience. In most cases, if you are asked to do a working interview, you will be given very little instruction and put right to the task as though it was just another day at work for you. For best practices review the 'Cold Call Interviews' section. Just remember, you are on stage every moment of the interview. Give a command performance from start to finish. It is also very important to establish a rapport with the interviewer. The final decision may be based more so on subjectivity than most other types of interviews.

Informational Interview

This is unlike all of the other types of interviews. In an Informational Interview you, the job seeker will initiate and set up the interview with someone within the corporation or industry that you are pursuing a position. This falls under the umbrella of networking and it really requires much the same skills as a sales person making a cold call. Even astute job seekers tend to leave this type of interview out of their job seeking regiment because they are either not aware of the process or if they are it may seem daunting.

For that reason, including this strategy into your job search process will give you an advantage over applicants that do not use this procedure. Seeking a dream job is a full time job and as with any job, the people that go the extra mile are more likely to be successful. In this type interview, the job seeker has much more control of the process and it is far less stressful because you are not seeking placement at this time, only information. In this process, you are the interviewer, therefore, it is also easier on the person you are interviewing due to the facts; 1) They will be flattered you are asking for their opinion and suggestions 2) They do not have to make a hiring decision on you when the interview is over.

You must be well organized and prepared to get all you can out of this opportunity. You still will need to do all of the preparation and research as you would for any other interview so you can prepare a list of the key questions you want to ask before you set up this meeting.

Two suggestions on how to set this type of interview up are, 1) You can visit a location of the corporation and seek out a contact. 2) You may place a call to the location and try to make a connection with a contact that you may meet with later. It is not a good idea to hold the interview itself by phone because your contact will most likely be more reluctant to speak openly with someone he or she cannot see or may become uneasy at some point of your questioning.

The purpose of this type of interview is to:
- **Network**
- **Get answers to a comprehensive list of questions you have prepared before hand**
- **Seek advice and insight from people working in the job you are seeking**
- **Get to know people in the industry or company**
- **Get leads on possible openings**
- **Get to know who makes the hiring decisions**
- **Get the names of possible contacts for later**
- **Find out what the company's expectations and priorities**
- **Build a relationship with the person you speak with so they may become a referral for you**

Cold Call (on site visit) Informational Interview

If you can, go visit the company that you would like to work for so you can get to see what the company is like and how they go about their normal day-to-day routine. During this visit, you are looking at the company through the eyes of a customer, client or patient according to what type of business. It is all right to make contact with associates of the company. As you go through this process, there are some critical things to stay focused on and to complete.

If there are several associates working when you get there, seek out the one that seems to be friendly and outgoing.

Once you make contact; remember you are imposing on not only his or her time but also the companies time so keep the visit as brief as possible while allowing enough time to reach your objectives.

Introduce yourself in an upbeat friendly way and it is a good idea to add a complement about the person or the business but only if it is a sincere complement. Important note, your complement should never be a personal one about the person; such as , I like the way your hair looks or those pants like great on you. Your complement should be along the lines of; your desk seems so well organized or, I could not help but over hear you speaking with that last customer and I just wanted to tell you I thought you handled that very well. Remember, we all enjoy recognition of a job well done and as you proceed through your task, he or she will feel a better connection to you and take an interest in sharing what information they can help you with.

Let him or her know you have an interest in joining the company and would appreciate any information they can share to help you better understand the company or the job. You will find most people will be more than happy to answer your questions and help you.

This is critical to your visit, know what you want to know. Make sure you have your basic four or five questions ready to go. Remember, you are working against the clock. You will have a brief window of opportunity to get all the information you need before he or she will have to go on with their duties or become uncomfortable with the process.

You will need to be quick and to the point. You will not have or take any notes until you leave, then you can write down any facts you need to record.

Lastly doing this visit, try to get the name of another person that could be a good contact for you, ideally, someone in a higher position of authority than the person you are speaking with.

Final Interview

If you are at the point of going on a final interview, congratulations may be in order. In this type of interview, the employer wants to hire you and will most likely use this meeting to clarify points or issues, for them and for you. First round interviews are rather broad in scope by design and interviewers are reluctant to give much insider information about the company until he or she is ready to hire you. In this interview, the interviewer will be looking to get more details about you and give you more specifics about the job. It is an opportunity for them to identify any problems missed in previous interviews that could keep you from getting the position. With all things being satisfactory, it can also be to make the job offer and cover the benefit and compensation packages. You should be prepared to negotiate.

Follow- up Interview

Follow-up interviews are part of a series of interviews and fall in the middle of the interview process. The progressing is as follows,

Phone interview
Main / first (face-to-face) interview

Follow-Up Interview

The purpose of the follow-up interview is to get more opinions on you to help decide if you would be the best candidate for the position. The interviewer will have a structured interview form with them. How much he or she will use the form will vary widely. The follow-up interview will not be as long as the first interview, on average about half as long. This interview can and will go in any direction, depending on the interviewer. The two top priorities of these interviews are, 1-) Ask follow-up questions to get to know you better and allow you an opportunity to ask more question yourself and 2-) Uncover any possible reasons not to hire you. It is important for you to try to determine rather the interviewer is focused on #1 or #2. If the interviewer seems focused on #1, just looking for clarification, that is good news and it should be easy to establish a rapport and feel free to ask whatever questions you may have. If the interviewer seems more focused on #2, looking for reasons not to hire you, it will be difficult to establish a rapport and he or she may even make the process feel more like a stress interview. In this case, keep your answers friendly, fact-based and brief.

Keep in mind a follow-up interview is good news, the further you go in the interview process the closer you are getting to the position you are seeking.

Blank page for your notes

CHAPTER 5

Preparing For the Interview

When you know the employer and position you will be interviewing for, put yourself in the employer's seat and focus on what they will be looking for. A great way to understand how to tailor your resume and answers to any interview question for the position you seek is to review any advertisements from the corporation about the position. Focus on the section that states the qualifications for the position. That will help you focus on the skills you have that fit their needs. Keep your focus on how you as a part of the team will help the corporation and not just on you.

When being interviewed, you are on stage and want to give a command performance. Therefore, you need to prepare for the interview just as you would prepare to give a speech or perform in anyway publicly. Your interview is a public performance.

Remember knowledge is power and information is knowledge so the more information you can get about the corporation you will be interviewing with, the more power you will have in the interview.

First, go on line to the business section and spend an hour or two reading all the reports and articles you can find on the company you are going to interview with. If it is a publicly held company, (listed on the stock market) review all the information you can about the stock price, where it is now, how it compares to its industry and biggest competitors. Review the corporation's fifty- two week stock price history, how much if any dividends were paid, and earnings per share and review all analyst reports. If you already follow the stock market, you probably know how to get all of this information. If you have never researched the financial information of a company, you will be pleasantly surprised at just how easy getting all of this information will be; in fact you can get all the facts from one business web page that will have links to all of the information you will want.

Next, go to the company's home web page where you will find a number of links that will give you even more information about the company such as, company officers, how the company feels about itself and the corporation's future plans. You may also find a job description with responsibilities and requirement for the position you are seeking. On this site, you will also find information about the company's products and services as well as any charitable ventures. As you research this information, a good practice is to read the documents, go back and review again this time pulling out the facts you need and writing them down.

Now your third step is to pull together all of your notes and construct an organized easy to use outline of all the information about the company you will need for your impressive interview. The reason for this process is to help get the facts ingrained in your thoughts about the corporation even before your outline is ready for use as a study guide.

The three steps;
- Read all the information you can find on the corporation
- Go back over the information and write down the key points you want to talk about
- Put together an organized outline of the facts to use as a study guide for your interview.

The amount of prepping and organization you will need to be successful in landing your dream job can be staggering but the information and the details about the corporation you will collect will help you better understand the job and what the corporation will expect from a successful candidate. Remember, the first and most difficult task you will have in any job is getting the job.

Blank page for your notes

Body Language

While you are orally answering interviewer's questions, your body may be saying something totally different.

Interviews are nerve racking. We all tend to react to nervous moments with some type of body movement; no matter how small or inconsequential it may seem to you, it may speak volumes to the interviewer. Controlling your body language is a skill. As with any skill you will become better at it with practice. Good non-verbal communication techniques are essential for a great interview. It is a good idea to do some mock interviews with someone you are close to or practice answering questions in front of a mirror. Here are some key points to consider.

Be on time, in fact be early, you should be waiting for the interviewer, the interviewer should never have to wait for you.

Be aware that your interview starts as you are approaching the building of the potential employer. Someone may just be looking out a window as you approach that may be involved in the interview or have some say in the final decision. You do not want them to see you exhibiting any behaviors you would not exhibit in the interview room.

This rule also applies at the end of your interview; remember as you are leaving it is not over until you are out of sight of the building. You may be on stage as you enter and exit so look at those times as part of your interview process.

All gestures, eye movement, facial expressions and posture are part of your body language. You must be very aware of what your body language is saying while you are talking.

Keep eye contact but do not stare, there is a fine line between the two. Your eyes can be very expressive; starring will come across as uninterested, bored and distant. Proper eye contact comes across as interested, enthusiastic and engaged.

When you first meet the interviewer, your handshake will be as memorable as your smile or lack of a smile. It should always be firm without causing discomfort to the interviewer. It should never leave the interviewer feeling like he or she just stuck their hand into a bowl of Jell-O.

When you take your seat, sit up straight, do not slouch in the chair and if you can, lean slightly forward in the chair, this shows your interest and enthusiasm. Never fold your arms across your chest, this come across as putting up a barrier, disinterested and arrogant.

Keep your hands away from your face at all times. Trained interviewers may read your touching any part of your face in a number of ways, most of them negative. From you not understanding, right up to what you are saying may not be true. A word to the wise, avoid touching your face during an interview.

Consistently answer all questions slowly and deliberately. This will give you time to think about what you are saying and once the interviewer gets use to your pace, when a more difficult question comes and you need the time to think, it will go unnoticed.

Dress code for interviewing is an extension of body language. You have undoubtedly heard the term "dress for success", that simply means dress as if you want the position. It is a good idea to get to know the official dress code of the corporation before you go to the interview. It is also acceptable to call ahead and ask, what is the corporation's expectation for dress code in an interview? Denims, tee shirts and flip-flops are not appropriate for an interview and of course, you must be neat and clean.

Body language is a fundamental part of the way all people communicate and differs by gender, society and nationality. My purpose here is not to try to get you to stop any movement while in an interview; I doubt any of us could do that and if we did, it would come across as weird or negative body language to the interviewer. My purpose here is to make sure you stay focused on sending the same message with body language as you are with your words.

Blank page for your notes

How to Answer Questions in an Interview

Answering interview questions effectively is a practiced skill. Once you have outlined your competencies / skills, completed your objective statement and your resume, composed your two minute elevator speech, identified the position you would like to apply for and have completed your informal interview, you are now ready to prepare for your interview.

Example question #1

A common question that may be asked in an interview is:

"Why do you want to work with this company"?

Answers that are sure to make it a short interview are:
- I saw you had an ad in the paper.
- I think I can do this type of work
- I need a job.

Due to all the information that you have gathered from your research and put into a powerful outline for reference, you will be able to work in names and facts about the company that will surely impress the interviewer. Your answer to that same question may be more like this:

Example of a well-constructed answer;

"As I looked into several companies that I thought I may be interested in working with, I was very much impressed with what your company has achieved and the direction you are going. John Smith, your CEO made some very positive comments about next year's growth. The company showed that you really care about the community by making a $XXX contribution to charities I know that 70% of your managers were promoted from within. I believe my skills set will fit in very well with this company.

Now that is an answer the interviewer will be very impressed with and will not forget.

Example question #2

Why do you think you are the best candidate for this position? The ideal way to answer this question would be to quote some of the qualifications one at a time directly from the ad for the position and link a skill or accomplishment from your resume to each qualification. This will be easy for you to do because of two key factors, 1-the extensive research you did on the company and the position you are seeking and 2- the understanding you have of your skills and accomplishment from the detailed work you did creating your resume and elevator speech. Your answer may go like this:

The position requires someone with five years of management experience; I had been a manager for the XYZ Company for nine years. You are looking for a manager that will be involved in staffing; I worked very closely with my human resource manager at the XYZ Company to make sure every position was filled with the right people as a result our turnover rate was 20% below the corporate rate for the last 3 years. Improving customer service is a key part of this position; I developed a customer service program that improved our customer service score from 82.4 to 91.3 for the year. Your position requires a leader that can control expenses. By focusing on and reviewing all controllable expanses, my team and I were able to reduce expenses by 12% last year, which added 8% right to our profit.

By answering questions in this manner, you are taking some control of the interview gently guiding it in the direction you want it to go. Here is how.

1-) Each part of you answer is predicated on what they are looking for,
2-) Each part of your answer tells the interviewer that you meet each of the qualifications.
3-) Your answer demonstrates a proven record of accomplishment.

Because of the facts you included by giving figures and percentages in your answer, the interviewer is likely to ask his or her next questions based on what you have put on the table. For instance, you said you "reduced expenses by 12%". That was what you did. A good interviewer will now want to know and will ask, how did you accomplish that achievement? Therefore, your skillful answering to his or her question will help keep the interview close to your comfort zone.

Included in this guide is an extensive list of questions you may receive in an interview. By following the same format as I used in answering the two example questions, you will do well in answering most interview questions.

Remember the true anatomy of an interview. The interviewer's job is to find the candidate that has the best knowledge of what the position requires, the best skill set to handle the position; the best-proven record of accomplishments and is the most enthusiastic about getting the position.

Blank page for your notes

Common Interview Questions

- How would your current or last boss describe you?
- How would your co-workers describe you?
- Tell me about your worst boss.
- Tell me about your best boss.
- Why did you leave your last job or want to leave your current job?
- Why do you want to work for this organization?
- What type of boss do you prefer to work for?
- What type of boss do you least like to work for?
- What do you see yourself doing in five years?
- What has been your greatest accomplishment so far?
- What has been your biggest failure so far?
- In your last evaluation, what areas did you receive your highest ratings?
- In your last evaluation, what areas were you rated as needs improvement?
- In what area do you really excel?
- What is your biggest weakness?
- What do you like about our organization?
- How do you feel you will help our organization?
- What makes a successful leader?
- How do you work with a difficult boss?
- How do you work with a difficult subordinate?
- What did you like most about you last job?
- What did you like least about your last job?
- What are your interests outside of work?
- What is your leadership style?
- What trends do you see in this business?
- What do you expect from this company?
- Are you honest?
- What makes you angry?
- What make you unique?
- What are your limitations?
- Tell me about a disagreement you had with your boss?
- What kind of decisions do you not like to make?
- How would you rate your last employer?
- What do you like to read?
- Do you work best with oral instructions or written instructions?
- How do you react to chance?
- What can you offer this organization?
- What would you do if your boss asked you to do something you totally disagree with?
- How do you work with high performing associates?
- How do you work with low performing associates?

The purpose of this section is not to give you the right answers or for that matter, to even suggest there are right or wrong answers. The purpose of this section is to make you think about how you would answer these questions so if they come up, you will give your best answer.

Blank page for your notes

CHAPTER 6

The Thank You Letter

The Thank You letter is a very important and straightforward document that should be included in your job-seeking package. You should send a Thank You Letter to the person that conducted the interview. This document serves three critical purposes. 1-) It shows good etiquette and that you really appreciated him or her taking time to meet with you. 2-) It keeps you front and center in the mind of the interviewer as he or she completes the process of making the hiring decision. 3-) It is another opportunity for you to ask for the job.

Example of a Thank You Letter

Your Street Address
City, State, Zip Code
Telephone Numbers
E-Mail Address

Mr. John Doe
XYZ Company
1234 Main St
New York, New York 24680

Thank you for taking so much time on Monday May 1st. to acquaint me with your company and the expectations of the position you are looking to fill. I was very impressed with the details you shared with me on all of the programs your company has in place to recognize and reward your associates; I can see why you retain so many of your employees. After further consideration of our conversation about the opportunity your company offers, I feel very strongly that my background and skills will be a definite asset in helping your company in reaching your objectives with minimal supervision. Mr. Doe, I am very much looking forward to hearing from you when you have made your hiring decision.

Regards,
Sign your name

Blank page for your notes

CHAPTER 7

Negotiating Starting Salaries

When the time comes to talk about starting salary and benefits, most job seekers turn into great listeners and very amenable, hoping for the best but most likely getting the average or below. Two very important points to remember once you have made it to a job offer. Job openings have two sides, the job seeker wants the job and the employer needs to fill the position with the best possible candidate.

This is a time you may influence an immediate pay increase that will also affect every increase you will get during your career with the corporation.

Here is the simple math, in most positions you will have an annual evaluation and may receive an increase that will be a percentage of your salary. For most of us, a 5 to 7% increase at our annually review would be something to celebrate. However, handling your negotiations properly may get you a 10 % or higher increase in your starting salary. A higher starting salary will mean a higher dollar increase every year. Here is an outline that will help negotiate your starting salary.

First, do the research on what the salary range is for the position.

Let the interviewer bring up the first salary number; this can be tough because you may be asked what your salary expectations are. In this case let the interviewer know you have done your research about the salary range of the company or industry. Add that you will be giving the organization 100% and expect in return a competitive starting salary. You should know the minimum that you will accept going in.

If the interviewer pushes you to give a salary range, do not give a large range, i.e., $50,000 to $65,000. It is better to give a shorter range, i.e. $60,000 to $65,000. This is because once you give your range, while you focus on the higher number, the interviewer will focus on the lower number.

Do not share the information you have from your research until after the numbers are on the table. If the offer is low, the information you have will be a very strong bargaining chip along with reemphasizing your qualifications as well as how you will execute or exceed corporate goals. Your strong resume will justify your worth.

Aside from being pushed into having to give numbers, stay vague on salary until you know for sure, there is a job offer on the table. Giving numbers too early or before the interviewer gives a salary range could have one of three consequences you may never know about. 1) You could end up with a lower starting salary then the company actually was prepared to give. 2) You could lowball yourself to the point you do not get the job because the interviewer thinks you are under qualified for the position. 3) If your number is way out of line on the high side, the interviewer may think you are not realistic and will not be satisfied with what the interviewer has to offer.

You may be thinking with the way things are for job seekers, should I go after all I can get? Yes... If you did the proper research and know the salary range for the position, do not be afraid to negotiate on the high side. People tend to think the higher the salary the more the company will expect from us. The truth is the expectations are attached to the position, not the salary. You will be required to reach the expectations and goals of the position no matter what starting salary you receive. Remember, the company is not hiring you as a favor to you; the company is hiring to fill a position that is important to the organization.

You should also have a good understanding of the company's benefits and career opportunities. A great benefit package or a sure opportunity to advance could mean much more to your financial future than the starting salary itself. Finally, never lose sight of the fact that this is a negotiation not an argument. Your goal is to convince the interviewer that increasing the offer would be the right decision and would benefit the company. Your goal is not to prove them wrong.

Blank page for your notes

SUMMARY

Hooray! A guide designed for baby boomers. After reading and following the practices in this guide, you are ready to go out and conquer the uncertainties of the job search.

Practice makes perfect. After you have put your total interview package together, it is critical that you practice your interviewing skills. You should practice being interviewed and practice playing the role of the interviewer as well. By playing the role of the interviewer you have to come up with questions to get at information you want to know about the candidate as an employer. You may come up with questions that you did not anticipate when practicing only how to answer questions. You can practice these mock interviews while looking in a mirror, using a tape recorder or with a family member or friend that you trust will work with you to help you improve. Mock interviews will identify points you need to work on such as,

- Important skills you want to be sure and communicate to the interviewer
- How to avoid giving information that may be unflattering about you
- Controlling the impulse to talk too much
- Controlling your body language and reaction to difficult questions
- Comfortably answering common questions with brief impactful stories that keep the interviewer thinking of how well you seem to fit their needs
- Focus on being able to quickly process questions for better understanding before you answer, and
- Gives you an opportunity to see yourself just as the interviewer may see you

Job-hunting is difficult at best. I have shared with you some comprehensive and vital information from A to Z on how to get your dream job. The information in this guide comes from years of research and interviewing on both sides of the table. I confidently make this bold statement, **'if you follow the procedures in this guide, you will absolutely do much better in your job pursuit'**. You now have all the information you need to successfully seek out and get, your dream job.

Good luck in controlling your career!

INDEX